D1355213

my first book of questions and answers

dinosaurs

Maggie Brown

p

This is a Parragon Book
First published in 2002

Parragon
Queen Street House
4 Queen Street
Bath BA1 1HE, UK

Copyright © Parragon 2002

Produced by

David West  Children's Books
7 Princeton Court
55 Felsham Road
Putney
London SW15 1AZ

British Library Cataloguing-in-Publication Data

A catalogue record for this book is available from the British Library.

Hardback ISBN 0-75257-564-3
Paperback ISBN 0-75257-570-8

Printed in China

Designers
Aarti Parmar, Rob Shone, Fiona Thorne

Illustrator
James Field (SGA)

Cartoonist
Peter Wilks (SGA)

Editor
James Pickering

CONTENTS

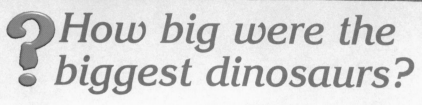

How big were the biggest dinosaurs?

Long-necked dinosaurs, such as Brachiosaurus, were massive. Measuring more than 22 m from head to tail, and weighing well over 30 tonnes, this dinosaur was about as long as a tennis court and heavier than five elephants. It was tall enough to peer over the top of a four-storey house!

Brachiosaurus

? How small were the smallest dinosaurs?

Some dinosaurs were tiny. At about 1 m long, for example, Compsognathus wasn't much larger than a turkey!

Compsognathus

Brachiosaurus was the biggest dinosaur of all.

FALSE. Other long-necked dinosaurs were even larger – Argentinosaurus may have been twice as big.

Dinosaurs were the biggest animals ever.

FALSE. The blue whale is the biggest animal ever, at 130 tonnes.

?How many kinds of dinosaur were there?

Dinosaurs were around for millions of years, and all sorts of different kinds developed. Scientists have now named about 800 dinosaurs, but there may have been twice as many kinds altogether.

When did dinosaurs live?

The very first kinds of dinosaur appeared on Earth about 225 million years ago. One of the earliest was Herrerasaurus, a meat-eater that lived in the area we now call Argentina.

What sort of animal were they?

Dinosaurs were reptiles, but they were a bit different from other reptiles such as lizards, crocodiles and tortoises. Dinosaurs held their legs straight under their bodies – unlike other reptiles, whose legs sprawl out to the side.

TRUE OR FALSE?

Dinosaurs could fly.

FALSE. They were land animals. Other creatures ruled the air and the seas.

Dinosaur babies hatched from eggs.

TRUE. Like other reptiles, dinosaurs laid eggs.

How do we know about dinosaurs?

No one knows exactly what dinosaurs were like because, about 65 million years ago, they all suddenly died out. Scientists work like detectives to piece bits of information together, and their main clues are fossils – the stony remains of living things that died a very long time ago.

How were fossils made?

Sometimes a dead animal would sink to the bottom of a river, lake or sea, where it was covered by sand or mud. Over millions of years, the sand and mud became rock, and the animal's bones turned into fossils.

What kind of dinosaur fossils do scientists find?

The most common dinosaur fossils formed from hard body parts such as bones and teeth. Sometimes, though, scientists find fossils of dinosaur eggs or droppings, or rocks that show the pattern of their skin or footprints.

Egg

Footprint

Tooth

?What did dinosaurs eat?

Most dinosaurs ate plants. There were lots of fierce and hungry meat-eaters, though, and they ate anything they could catch, including other dinosaurs!

Pine-trees

Ginkgo

Magnolia

Why do scientists love dinosaur droppings?

It's lucky that fossils don't smell, because scientists study fossilised dinosaur droppings to find out about the kind of things dinosaurs liked to eat.

Cycad

Did dinosaurs eat grass?

No, not even plant-eating dinosaurs ate grass, because these plants didn't appear until long after the dinosaurs died out. Plant-eating dinosaurs mainly ate ferns and early kinds of tree, such as the palm-like cycad, and pine trees.

Who was king of the dinosaurs?

Rex means 'king', and Tyrannosaurus means 'tyrant lizard' (a tyrant is a cruel, powerful ruler). Scientists named Tyrannosaurus rex because they thought it was big and mean enough to rule over all other animals, killing and eating anything it fancied. At about 12 m, it was bus-sized, with a huge head and a mouth big enough to gulp you down whole.

Tyrannosaurus rex

?What colour was Tyrannosaurus?

No one has found a fossil that shows what colour any of the dinosaurs were. Scientists think that some were brightly coloured, while others were patterned to match their surroundings – just as many animals are today.

Giganotosaurus

?Who was the giant dinosaur?

Giganotosaurus means 'giant southern lizard', and scientists think that this meat-eater was even bigger than Tyrannosaurus!

TRUE OR FALSE?

Tyrannosaurus could run as fast as a car.

FALSE. No dinosaurs could run that fast, but Tyrannosaurus could still have run a lot faster than you do!

Tyrannosaurus left enormous droppings.

TRUE. Scientists have found a fossil of a loaf-sized dropping, which probably came from a Tyrannosaurus.

❓ *Which dinosaur went fishing?*

At about 10.5 m long, Baryonyx was a big dinosaur with crocodile-like jaws. Scientists think it ate fish, snapping them up in its mouth or hooking them up out of the water with its thumb claws, just as grizzly bears do today.

Baryonyx

Suchomimus

Which dinosaur had a sail on its back?

No one is certain what the sail-like structure on Spinosaurus's back was for. It may have been used like a flag to signal to other dinosaurs, or it may have worked a bit like a solar panel to help Spinosaurus heat up or cool down.

Spinosaurus

Who was the biggest fish-eater?

Suchomimus was at least a metre longer than its cousin Baryonyx, and probably grew to as long as the 12-m Tyrannosaurus.

? Which dinosaur had a long big toenail?

Velociraptor was one of the scariest dinosaurs in the 1993 movie Jurassic Park. This dinosaur didn't just have sharp teeth and vicious clawed hands. Even more frightening was the huge curved claw on each foot – when Velociraptor attacked, it could swing these claws forwards, to slash at its prey.

Velociraptors

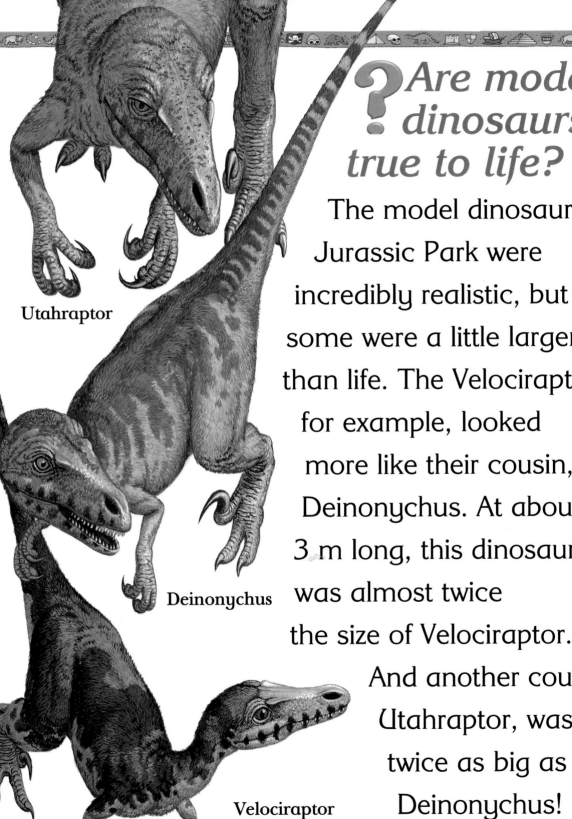

Utahraptor

Deinonychus

Velociraptor

❓ *Are model dinosaurs true to life?*

The model dinosaurs in Jurassic Park were incredibly realistic, but some were a little larger than life. The Velociraptors, for example, looked more like their cousin, Deinonychus. At about 3 m long, this dinosaur was almost twice the size of Velociraptor. And another cousin, Utahraptor, was twice as big as Deinonychus!

Velociraptor and its cousins used to hunt in packs.

TRUE. It helped them to kill dinosaurs a lot bigger than themselves.

Only these sorts of dinosaur were pack hunters.

FALSE. Other meat-eating dinosaurs, such as Coelophysis, also hunted in packs.

Diplodocus

❓Which dinosaurs cracked a whip?

The huge plant-eating dinosaurs didn't just have long necks – some of them also had incredibly long tails. Apatosaurus, Barosaurus and Diplodocus may have flicked their extra-long tails like a whip, making an incredibly loud noise to scare away their enemies.

Allosaurus

? Why did the long-necked dinosaurs eat stones?

The long-necked dinosaurs couldn't chew their tough plant food. To get at the goodness, they swallowed stones which rubbed together in their tummies to mash the plants into a mush.

Brain

Stomach

? Were long-necked dinosaurs brainy?

The long-necked dinosaurs had tiny brains in comparison to their huge bodies. Because of this, scientists think they were among the least intelligent of the dinosaurs.

Long-necked dinosaurs were very greedy.

TRUE. They were so big that to stay alive, they had to spend nearly all their time eating.

Tyrannosaurus rex was the brainiest dinosaur.

FALSE. It was brainier than long-necked dinosaurs, but not as smart as a Velociraptor.

?Which dinosaurs had duckbills?

Parasaurolophus, Corythosaurus and Lambeosaurus belonged to a group of plant-eating dinosaurs called duckbills – named because their mouths ended in a toothless beak, or bill. When predators threatened them, they could run away on two legs, and may have rushed into the water to escape.

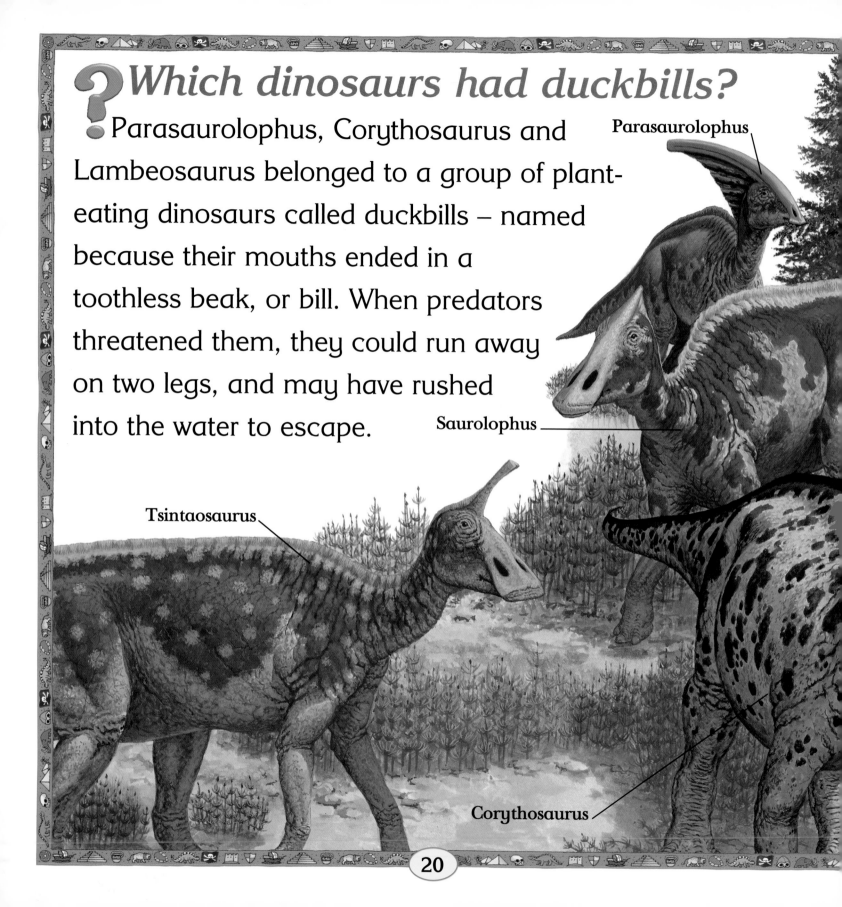

Parasaurolophus

Saurolophus

Tsintaosaurus

Corythosaurus

? Who liked to blow his own trumpet?

Parasaurolophus had a weird, hollow crest bone, which it may have blown through like a trumpet. Scientists made a model of the bone, and found it produced a low booming sound.

Air space

Lambeosaurus

? Who was the helmet lizard?

Corythosaurus means 'helmet lizard', even though this dinosaur's crest looked more like a dinner plate than a helmet! Scientists think the duckbilled dinosaurs used their crests to show off when trying to attract a mate.

?Were dinosaurs good parents?

Maiasaura means 'good mother lizard', and scientists named this dinosaur because they found it beside a nest full of its babies. Other kinds of dinosaur may have also stayed with their young, feeding and protecting them.

Maiasaura

?Which dinosaur laid the biggest egg?

Some of the biggest eggs found so far belonged to a long-necked dinosaur called Hypselosaurus. They were about 30 cm long – roughly the same size as a rugby ball.

Oviraptor

❓ Which of the dinosaurs was an egg robber?

Oviraptor means 'egg robber', and this dinosaur also got its name because it was discovered near a nest. Scientists used to think it was about to steal the eggs when it died. Later they found a fossilised Oviraptor that had died protecting its own nest, proving it was a good parent, after all.

? Why did Triceratops have horns?

Triceratops was like a giant rhinoceros – as heavy as an elephant and as long as a truck. Even though it looked so fierce, Triceratops was a plant-eater and probably used its horns to scare off meat-eating enemies, such as Tyrannosaurus rex and Velociraptor.

Triceratops

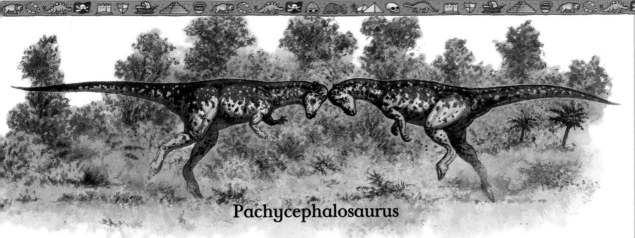

Pachycephalosaurus

Who were headbangers?

Pachycephalosaurus's skull was so thick and tough that scientists think it worked like a crash helmet, and that these dinosaurs fought each other by headbanging.

Pentaceratops

Which dinosaur was a bighead?

Triceratops's head was about 2 m long, but its cousin Pentaceratops's was bigger. At over 3 m, even a car could have parked on it!

? Why were some dinosaurs built like tanks?

Hylaeosaurus

Some plant-eating dinosaurs, such as Sauropelta, were big bruisers with extra-tough skin covered in bony spikes and bumps. All this armour-plating helped protect them against meat-eaters.

Polacanthus

Sauropelta

? Which dinosaur spiked its enemies?

Stegosaurus's tail had vicious spikes at its tip, which were just as dangerous as Triceratops's horns.

Stegosaurus

? Which dinosaur packed a mean punch?

When Euoplocephalus swung its tail, the bumps on its tip worked like a club for bashing its enemies about Ouch!

? How fast could dinosaurs run?

Scientists think that dinosaurs such as Gallimimus and Struthiomimus were the speediest, and that they could run as fast as ostriches. Ostriches can't fly, but they are the largest birds alive today – with their long, strong legs they can belt across the ground at speeds of up to 65 kph.

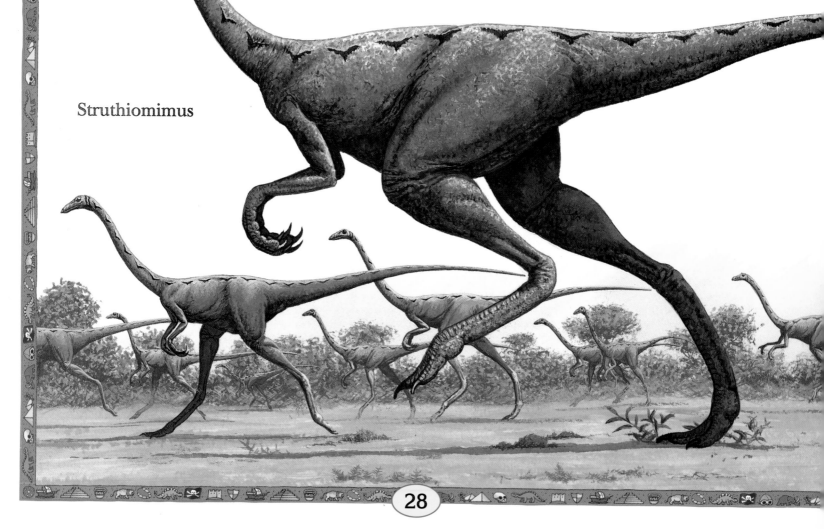

Struthiomimus

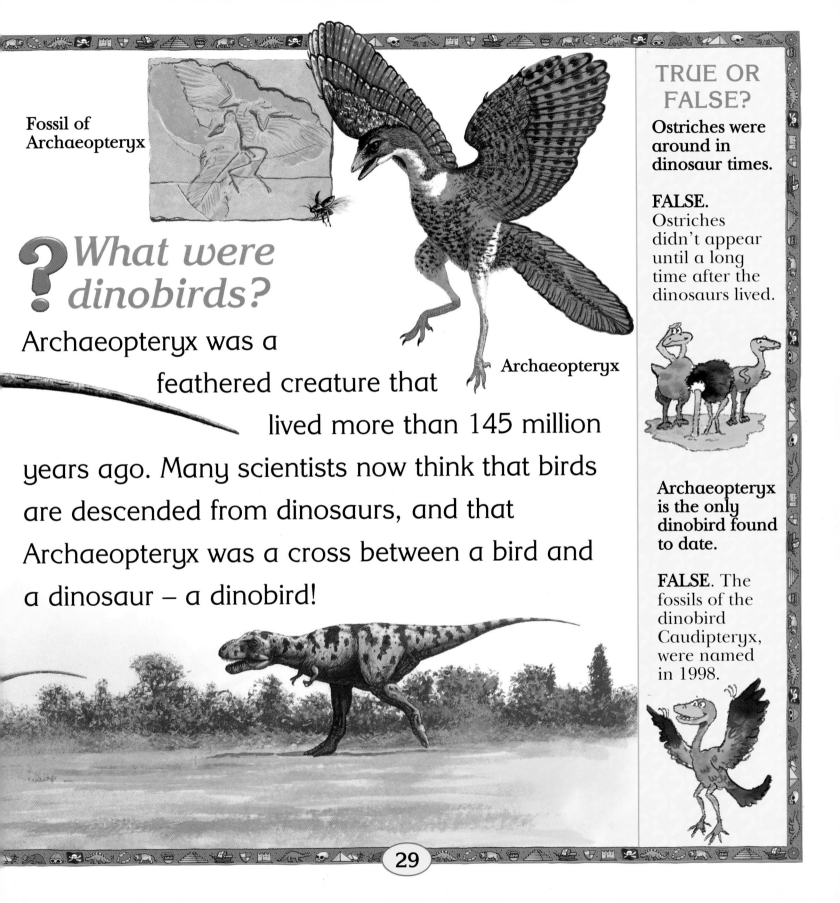

Fossil of
Archaeopteryx

?*What were dinobirds?*

Archaeopteryx

Archaeopteryx was a feathered creature that lived more than 145 million years ago. Many scientists now think that birds are descended from dinosaurs, and that Archaeopteryx was a cross between a bird and a dinosaur – a dinobird!

TRUE OR FALSE?

Ostriches were around in dinosaur times.

FALSE. Ostriches didn't appear until a long time after the dinosaurs lived.

Archaeopteryx is the only dinobird found to date.

FALSE. The fossils of the dinobird Caudipteryx, were named in 1998.

What happened to the dinosaurs?

Many scientists think that 65 million years ago,
a gigantic chunk of space rock smashed into
the Earth. The force of the hit was like an
explosion. It threw up huge clouds of dust
which blocked out the Sun and plunged
the Earth into freezing darkness. Without
sunlight, plants couldn't grow, so first
the plant-eating dinosaurs died of
cold and hunger, then the
meat-eaters starved.

?Are any dinosaurs alive today?

Robin

No dinosaurs survived the disaster, but some birds did. So if scientists are right, and birds are descended from dinosaurs, then their relatives are still alive and hopping today!

Index